DEVON RIVIERA
— MOODS —

DEVON RIVIERA
MOODS

Photography by
KEVIN COWELL

HALSGROVE

First published in Great Britain in 2003

British Library Cataloguing-in-Publication Data
A CIP record for this title is available from the British Library

ISBN 1 84114 257 3

HALSGROVE

Halsgrove House
Lower Moor Way
Tiverton, Devon EX16 6SS
Tel: 01884 243242
Fax:01884 243325
email: sales@halsgrove.com
website: www.halsgrove.com

Printed by D'Auria Industrie Grafiche Spa, Italy

The English Riviera and its surrounding area is one of the most beautiful in the United Kingdom. Those of us who are fortunate enough to live here sometimes take it for granted, taking little time to appreciate the beauty of the landscape around us. The visitor, however, will have a different problem: often they will simply not have time to see every place of interest, or to experience the different moods that the weather creates throughout the seasons.

The shape of the landscape is also ever changing. Nature exerts her influence not only in the way the scenery is lit, but through the elements of wind, water and the sun. The English Riviera is blessed with wonderful beaches and a coastline sculpted over millions of years. Man, too, has influenced the shape of the land through the building of towns and villages, all of which is our part of our heritage.

Living and working in the Torbay area all my life I discovered that it is far more of a challenge to photograph your own backyard. It was necessary for me to look anew at the landscape in order to capture its essential qualities. My aim in this book has been to provide, for resident and visitor alike, a lasting portrait of the English Riviera and its dramatic coastal scenery. I hope everyone will find something here to remind them of their own favourite places, whether it be a glorious sunset at Brixham, a sunrise at Paignton Beach, a breaking wave at Torquay, a misty morning at Man Sands, or a summer afternoon's sailing at Salcombe.

Kevin Cowell
Torquay 2003

SOMERSET

DEVON

Dartmoor
National Park

CORNWALL

DETAIL

River Teign

River Bovey

Tottiford
Reservoir

Grimspound

Trenchford
Reservoir

Hound Tor

Bovey Tracey

Haytor

Widecombe-in-the-Moor

Bishopsteignton

Teignmouth

River Teign

Shaldon

Combeinteignhead

Dartmoor
National
Park

Babbacombe
Bay

Cockington

Torquay

Hope's Nose

Paignton

Churston

Totnes

Brixham

Berry Head

Kingswear

River Dart

Scabbacombe

Dartmouth

Outer Froward
Point

Inner
Froward
Point

Blackpool Sands

Slapton

Kingsbridge

Torcross

East Portlemouth

Salcombe

Start Point

Bolt Head

Lannacombe Bay

Prawle Point

To Tracy
(16.07.65–15.02.88)

ACKNOWLEDGEMENTS

On our life's journey we meet people from all walks of life – sometimes briefly, while at other times lasting relationships are formed. Each and every meeting, however brief or long will in some way have an influence on our character and direction in life. It is, therefore, difficult to acknowledge and thank each person individually, who has taught me, given advice and motivated me to reach the point where I am now. However, if you are reading this and have met or know me, I thank you.

A big thank-you to my wife Mandy, and children Samantha and Adam, for their patience and support particularly when I have been out photographing images for this book. I wish to thank my parents, they started my life's journey and without them this book would not have been conceived.

Also thanks to Simon and staff at Halsgrove for giving me the opportunity to produce this book and realise a goal. Many thanks in particular to Ken Duncan for his inspiration, Jane, Gary, David, Rob, Simon, Carl, Leigh and Jacky, for their motivation and conversations long into the night, with many glasses of Australian wine.

If you would like a print of these beautiful images or are interested in tuition, Kevin can be contacted either by email kevin@kevincowellphoto.co.uk or via the website www.kevincowellphoto.co.uk

THE PHOTOGRAPHS

Early morning, Teignmouth Beach

Sunrise at Teignmouth

Waves break against the sea wall at Teignmouth

The early train, Teignmouth

Stormy sky over Teignmouth

Opposite, top: *The Parson and Clerk at dawn, Teignmouth*

Below: *The Ness from Teignmouth*

No. 15 moored at Shaldon

Opposite: *Teignmouth from The Ness*

Sunrise on the Teign

Swans on the Teign

Sunset at Combeinteignhead

Opposite, top: *River Teign*

Below: *River Teign with flooded fields after heavy rain*

Bishopsteignton from Arch Brook Bridge

Metallic sea and sky over Babbacombe Bay

Babbacombe Bay

Sunrise at Fishcombe, Torquay

Overleaf: *New day at Thatcher Rock, Torquay*

Blackball Rocks, Oddicombe, Torquay

Hope's Nose, Torquay

Stormy sea off Hope's Nose, Torquay

Dawn at Meadfoot Beach, Torquay

Torquay Harbour

Diamond light, Torquay

Twilight, Torquay

Opposite, top: *New Year's Day, Torquay*

Below: *Dusk, Torquay*

Overleaf: *Livermead, Torquay*

London Bridge, Torquay

Torquay Harbour

Torquay Pier

A summer's day at the beach, Torquay

Torquay Inner Harbour

Opposite, top: *Boats in the evening light*

Below: *Reflections, Torquay Harbour*

Overleaf: *Torquay Harbour*

Evening light, Torquay Marina

Riviera dance, Torquay

Gardens on Torquay sea front

Evening spring sunshine at Cockington

Beautiful sky over Torquay, from Paignton

Opposite, top: *Blossom in spring sunshine, Cockington*

Below: *Flowers bloom at Cockington*

A battle of the elements, Paignton

Stormy seas pound the sea wall at Paignton

Above and opposite: *Reflections at Paignton Harbour*

Merry-go-round at Paignton

Opposite, top: *Fairground at Paignton*

Below: *Paignton Regatta fireworks*

Overleaf: *A new day, Paignton Beach*

Paignton Harbour

Sunrise at Paignton

Overleaf: *Preston Sands, Paignton*

Broadsands Beach, Churston

Rocks off Elberry, Churston

Breakwater at Brixham

Opposite: *Elberry Cove, Churston*

Berry Head, Brixham

Opposite, top: *Berry Head Lighthouse, Brixham*

Below: *The Fort at Berry Head, Brixham*

The lifeboat at Brixham

Opposite, top: Western Lady *at Brixham in the summer*

Below: *Boats moored at Brixham*

Brixham Harbour

Golden Hind, *Brixham*

A glorious sunset at Brixham

Rocks off Shoalstone, Brixham

St Mary's Bay, Brixham

Mist on Southdown Cliff, Man Sands

Above and opposite: *Water cascades down the cliffs at Scabbacombe*

Early morning, looking across to Pudcombe Cove

Early morning at Old Mill Bay

Hawthorn and gorse on the cliffs at Inner Froward Point

Opposite: *Daymark (a navigational aid), Coleton Fishacre*

Overleaf: *Boats sailing in the spring sunshine, Outer Froward Point*

Western Lady *moored at Galmpton Creek, winter*

Kingswear from Dartmouth

Overleaf: *Marina at Kingswear*

Steam train leaving Kingswear

Opposite: *Kingswear from Dartmouth*

Overleaf: *Dart Estuary*

Fireworks at the Dartmouth Regatta

The sun sets over Dartmouth

Dartmouth

Rape field, Little Dartmouth

Boats on the Dart at Totnes

Spring, Blackpool Sands

Summer, Blackpool Sands

A fiery dawn sky, Slapton

Moonrise at Slapton Beach

A boat on the beach at Slapton

Overleaf: *Slapton Beach*

Slapton

Dawn at Slapton Ley

Slapton Ley

Pink clouds reflect in the Ley at Slapton as the sun sets behind

Dawn at Torcross with the protective light of Start Point Lighthouse flashing for the last time that night

Early morning, Torcross

Overleaf: *Beach hut details*

Start Point Lighthouse

Cliffs at Start Point

Rough seas at Lannacombe Bay

Prawle Point

A blustery day at Portlemouth Down

Bluebells, East Portlemouth

Kingsbridge Estuary from East Portlemouth

Misty morning, Kingsbridge

Boats sailing on a summer afternoon, Salcombe

Salcombe from Sharp Tor

South Sands, Salcombe

Hut near East Soar Farm, Bolt Head

Beech wood in autumn, Bovey Tracey

Shadows of leaves on a tree, Bovey Tracey

Above and opposite: *Autumn reflections, River Bovey*

Lovely shades of green reflect in the calm summer water, River Teign

Sunrise at Haytor looking over the Teign Valley, Dartmoor

Overleaf: *Rock details and textures*

Haytor in the light of dawn, Dartmoor

Previous page: *Dartmoor in winter*

Widecombe-in-the-Moor, Dartmoor

Winter at Grimspound, Dartmoor

Snow scene looking towards Hound Tor, Dartmoor

Trenchford Reservoir, on the edge of Dartmoor

Tottiford Reservoir, on the edge of Dartmoor

Looking towards Dartmoor from Torquay. A balloonist quietly decends with the setting sun